11.50

DATE DUE

OCT 1 9 '77			

Let's Wonder About Science
LIQUID TO GAS AND BACK

J.M. Patten, Ed.D.

The Rourke Book Co., Inc.
Vero Beach, Florida 32964

9596

PHOTO CREDITS
All photos © J.M. Patten

Library of Congress Cataloging-in-Publication Data

Patten, J.M., 1944-
    Liquid to gas and back / J.M. Patten.
    p. cm. — (Let's wonder about science)
    Includes index.
    ISBN 1-55916-129-9
    1. Evaporation—Juvenile literature. 2. Condensation—Juvenile
literature. [1. Evaporation. 2. Condensation. 3. Air. 4. Water.] I. Title.
II. Series: Patten, J.M., 1944- Let's wonder about science.
QC304.P42   1995
536.4—dc20   95-6214
                                                                        CIP
                                                                         AC

Printed in the USA

TABLE OF CONTENTS

WHAT IS SCIENCE?

Evaporation and **condensation** are special science magic. They are two things young scientists enjoy watching and reading about.

Evaporation and condensation are mostly about water, which is always fun. You will find out how water seems to disappear, why it comes back again, and how rain is made.

Let's read all about the drying and dripping called evaporation and condensation.

Children make good scientists because they ask a lot of questions.

HEAT IS THE SECRET

Science is super amazing stuff. It can explain why puddles disappear and why soaking wet bathing suits dry in a flash. Science is the "magic" that fogs up your bathroom mirror while you're in the shower, and makes the outside of a cold glass of soda pop wet and slippery.

This puddle will disappear because of evaporation.

Condensation fogs up mirrors in steamy bathrooms.

Evaporation is what makes puddles disappear and bathing suits dry. Condensation puts fog on your mirror and drops of water on your glass. Evaporation and condensation explain why lots of things happen with water.

Let's take a closer look at how all this works. Here's a clue—the secret word is heat.

WATER CHANGES FORMS

Water can be in three **states,** or forms. Its solid form is ice, its liquid form is water, and its gaseous form is mist, steam or **water vapor.**

What is an ice cube like when you take it out of the freezer? Take a look—it's cold, hard and has a shape—an ice cube shape. This is the solid form of water.

If you take the ice cube outside on a sunny afternoon, what happens? Of course, it melts. Your piece of ice changes into a puddle of water.

Heat energy from the sun warms the particles, or tiny parts, that make up the ice. As the particles heat up, they begin dancing around and spreading out. When heat makes them go fast enough, the solid ice loses its shape—and turns into a puddle of water.

What will happen to these ice cubes out in the hot sun?

EVAPORATION—LIQUID TO GAS

Now the sun really heats up the little puddle of water. The water particles begin to move faster and faster, and spread farther and farther apart. As the temperature rises, the puddle starts to get smaller. Some of the water disappears. So where does the puddle go?

The tiny water particles, all heated up, move fast enough to jump out of the puddle and into the air as gas. This is called evaporation. Scientists say evaporation happens when heated liquid turns into **vapor,** or a gas, in the air.

How do we know the water is evaporating? We can see the puddle getting smaller and smaller—until its spot is dry.

The water level in this fish tank is getting lower because water is evaporating into the air.

EVAPORATION ALL AROUND US

Evaporation happens all around us. Let's look at ways evaporation helps us every day.

Do you have wet clothes? Hang them outside and they'll dry. Heat from the sun makes the water in your clothes turn into water vapor in the air. The hotter the day, the faster they'll dry.

These clothes will dry quickly on a hot day because heat speeds up evaporation.

Sweat helps keep our bodies cool during exercise.

Heat makes evaporation speed up.

Evaporation helps our bodies stay cool. When it gets hot, we begin to **perspire,** or sweat. The liquid sweat evaporates into the air, making our skin feel cooler.

Here's a question. Why, after a rainstorm, doesn't the road stay wet forever? Evaporation, of course, is the answer.

CONDENSATION—GAS TO LIQUID

We know that liquids turn into gases by evaporating. Can the opposite happen, too? Can a gas turn into a liquid? The answer is yes—it's called condensation.

Imagine you'd like to have a cold drink. First, take lots of ice cubes and place them in a tall glass. Pour your soda pop over the ice.

Okay—time for science—time to run around the block. That's right, put your soda pop down and go out and play for a bit, or read a book or do some homework.

Now come back and look at your glass. Do you notice anything different? Sure, the outside of your glass has little drops of water all over it.

Where did the water come from?

What will happen to this cold glass as it sits out in the sun?

DRIP, DRIP, DRIP— CONDENSATION

Condensation is when a gas changes into a liquid. Condensation is the opposite of evaporation.

The particles that make up gases are wild and crazy little guys. They have lots of heat energy and move about very, very fast. They stay far apart from each other, too. However, there is a way to slow these fellows down and make them stick closer together. Cool them off.

That's what happened to your cold glass of soda pop. Some of the water vapor—a gas in the air— got a little too close to the outside of that very cold glass.

The gas particles cooled, slowed down and came closer together. Their heat energy was taken away. Then it happened—the water vapor changed into liquid form. That's the wetness on the outside of your glass. That's condensation! Isn't science amazing?

As warm air hits a cold car, condensation forms.

EVAPORATION AND CONDENSATION WORK TOGETHER

Evaporation and condensation go hand in hand, like peanut butter and jelly. Let's see how they work together to do a very important job in nature.

Most of the water on Earth is salty ocean water that is not good to drink.

This lake in Vermont holds fresh water that will be used for drinking.

There is lots of water on the planet Earth—oceans, rivers, lakes, streams, ponds and even puddles. However, most of it is ocean water and too salty to drink. Only a small amount of our water is fresh and good to drink. Much of this water is ice at the north and south poles—which is pretty hard to swallow.

Nature is amazing. It takes the Earth's water and, through evaporation and condensation, turns it into water we can drink. Scientists call this the **water cycle.** Let's find out how it works.

THE WATER CYCLE

Nature stores most of the Earth's water in oceans and bodies of fresh water. Some water is in huge underground pools that are filled by rain seeping through the soil.

Heat from the sun warms the top layers of water above the ground. Some water evaporates and turns into water vapor. Water vapor is one of the gases in the air. When ocean water evaporates, its salt is left behind.

Next, the water vapor rises in the sky and cools down. Then, condensation turns the water vapor back to drops of water. These drops form clouds.

When too many water droplets gather, the cloud can't hold all of them. Some fall back to Earth as fresh, life-giving rain. Evaporation and condensation work together to make this happen.

These clouds hold water droplets that will fall back to Earth as rain.

GLOSSARY

condensation (kahn den SAY shun) — the process by which a gas changes into a liquid

evaporation (ee vap or AY shun) — the process by which a liquid changes into a gas

heat energy (HEET EN ur jee) — speeds up the movement of the particles that make up matter

perspire (per SPYR) — to sweat

states (STAYTS) — the forms of matter—solid, liquid and gas

vapor (VAY per) — matter in the form of a gas

water cycle (WAH ter SY kuhl) — the process in nature that turns the Earth's water into water we can drink

water vapor (WAH ter VAY per) — water in the form of a gas

The sun warms the water, and begins the water cycle.

INDEX